Bible Animals

An Early Learning Sticker Book • Written by Donna Cooner, Ed.D. • Illustrated by Rusty Fletcher

BROADMAN
& HOLMAN
PUBLISHERS

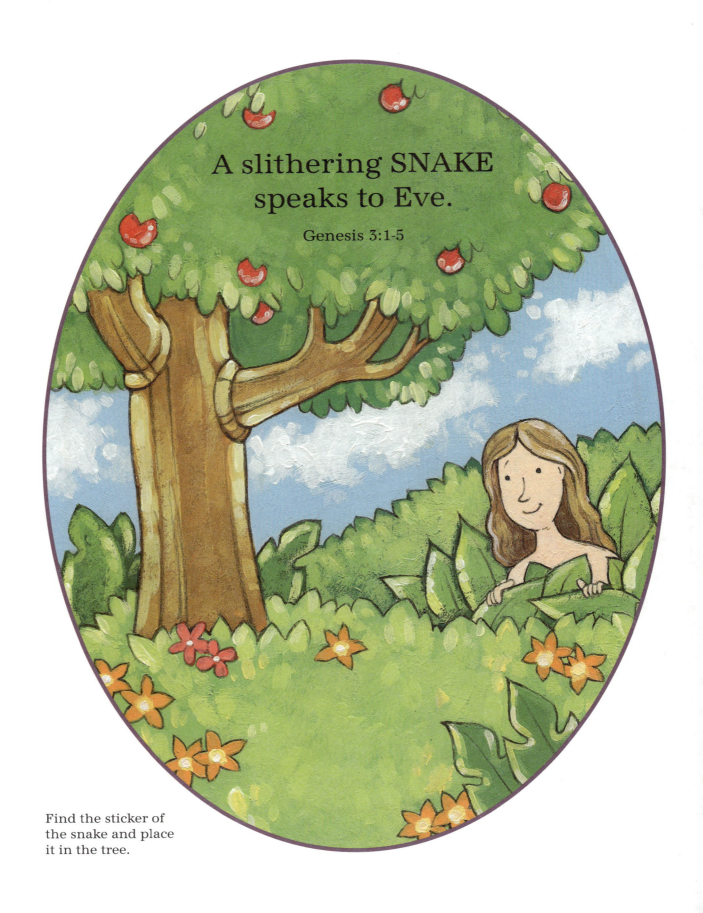

Rebekah cares for Abraham's CAMELS.

Genesis 24:12-23

Find camel stickers and place them near the trough.

Find cow stickers and place them on the river bank.

A stubborn DONKEY surprises Balaam by speaking.

Numbers 22:21-35

Find the sticker of the donkey and place it on the path.

Find the sticker of the bear and place it in front of David.

Find raven stickers and place them around Elijah.

Find lion stickers and place them near Daniel.

Find the sticker of the whale and place it in the sea.

A DOVE flies down to deliver God's message.

Matthew 3:16

Find the sticker of the dove and place it in the sky.

Find the sticker of the sheep and place it among the bushes.

Find the sticker of the colt and place it next to Jesus.

Find stickers of animal pairs and place them in line.